Unbreakable

LIKE A PHOENIX SHE ROSE FROM THE ASHES

ASHLEY VAUGHN WEST | UPLAND AVENUE

Printed in the United States of America Publisher: Upland Avenue Productions Author: Ashley Vaughn West ISBN-13: 978-1-7324167-9-6

DEDICATION

I want to dedicate this book to my two angels. Our love is
UNBREAKABLE!

Foreword

This book is about the unbreakable soul of a woman who refuses to give up. The word "Unbreakable" means being able to withstand an attempt to break. The author wrote this book as an attempt to show readers that with God all things are possible. As a child, it was always instilled in the author that "it doesn't matter how many times you fall but what matters is how many times you get back up."

Each poem that was written was a journey she had to heal, it was no going around it but through it. Let us remember the power of God is with you through all situations, protecting and strengthening you. Take peace and comfort in knowing that in Christ Jesus we are unbreakable in his power. The author's aspiration for writing this book is to bestow upon the reader or the world something that will be useful in times of need, depression, and discouragement. Times when you encounter a situation that makes you want to pull back from society to protect yourself or those you love. The unbreakable woman is a woman with strong faith and with that, she found comfort and strength in it. This strong woman has strength enough for the journey knowing that the journey is where she became strong.

"A promise that God has a plan for our lives and regardless of our current situation He can work through it to prosper us and give us hope."

Jeremiah 29.11

O. Pat Vaughn

UNBREAKABLE

Preface

I wrote this collection of poetry and spoken word to leave my imprint on the world. The words in this collection are depictions of experiences I have encountered or witnessed. These experiences and events compelled me to write. I've always known that paper is more patient than people. I've always been allured by the flow and the rhythm that poetry possesses with only the presence of mere words. It was my admiration for the craft and art of poetry that inspired me to write as a release and as a way to seek insight. I share my most intimate thoughts on life, love, faith, social issues, adversity, and rising from the ashes.

People like Paul Laurence Dunbar, Claude McKay, Zora Neale Hurston, Tupac Shakur, Lorraine Hansberry, Walt Whitman, Langston Hughes, Nina Simone, and Gil Scott Heron who used writing as a way of expressing social issues are sources of my inspiration. We have strayed away from the impact that literary writing has on society or how it records a specific time and captures its essence for future generations. Throughout history, there have been significant figures responsible for passing down history through stories or folklore like bards and griots. I am confident that years from now a person will pick up this book and it will reflect the milieu of where we are as a people today.

How Have You Been

When people ask, "How have you been?"
I reply, "I've been fine."
Thinking, if only you knew what is on my mind.
What I really should say is:
I've been praying for the Lord's protection.
Asking that He guides my steps.
I've been breaking generational curses.
I lost loved ones, so I've been riding in family hearses.
I've been breaking glass ceilings.
Pushing forward and ignoring feelings.
I've been fighting adversity.
Climbing corporate ladders, adding diversity.
I've been seeking clarity.
Reviving my creativity.
Manifesting visions.
I've been watching my people die on the television.
When stiff branches and nooses turn into bullets
And white sheets turn into blue badges.
While innocent people turn into hashtags.
So, I've been staying alive.
I've been changed, transformed, and set free.[1]
I've been learning to be a new me.

---

[1] Sarah Jakes Roberts

Table of Contents

ALLOW ME TO INTRODUCE ME TO MYSELF...

God said first, "let there be light"
Then He bestowed upon me the gift to write
To right the wrongs of the world, so that knowledge unfurls
Leaving no mind trapped by the bars of ignorance or
mediocrity
So I write to erase hypocrisy
To free minds from captivity

I AM

I am as beautiful as a pedal of a rose
I am the path in life that I chose
I move, speak, and breathe what I feel
Even if what I feel is ill
I still show no shield

I am alert even when you think I'm not
I am observing even when you think I've stopped
I am gracefully
Definitely
Never predictable

Outstandingly incredible
Divisible by none

There is no category for me because I am what I am and I
have done what I have done

BRILLIANCE TO INSANITY

I sway back and forth from brilliance to insanity
So caught up in the vanity
People lose all sense of humanity

Great thinkers suffer in a world that celebrates ignorance
One where all originality is sacrificed for a price

Some say imitation is the highest form of flattery but if the
imitator does not acknowledge from whom they borrow

Imitation can be the object of sorrow

Today minds are confined and easily led astray with
delusional thoughts of thinking, they made it on their own
so they feel there is no need to pray

Here I stand oscillating from brilliance to insanity

The Bible says the meek shall inherit the earth
But who will the world be given to if no man understands
its worth?

So, focused on themselves and the superficial
Real acts of kindness are at their dismissal

Modesty dies where hubris resides

The wise man says nothing while a fool tells it all
He talks of materialism but from his mouth wisdom never
falls
Never realizing that you can't impress a person who
equates value on things that can't be measured

While the fool goes home lonely
Cuddling cold lifeless treasures
Placing more esteem on things instead of beings

Crucifying authenticity
The real will remain buried in obscurity
Because they fear the potency of purity

As I sway back and forth from brilliance to my insanity

DOPE

I'm too woke to choke
Can't be an addict to the system because I'm too dope
Thoughts keep you afloat and ignorance makes you sink
Don't hurt yourself trying to think

My eyes are open to the fake
I don't even blink
Snakes smile at me
I give them a wink
Never saying a peep
If you think I'm blind to reality, then you're the one that's asleep

Nothing comes to a dreamer but dreams
So I'm up grinding sewing plans together by the seams
Showing my children how to be kings and queens

No bandwagon in me
I'm always rooting for the same team
Some minds are dirty but I try to keep my mind clean by staying
goal-oriented and never driven by the green

I am too dope to choke

My potent thoughts clog your lungs like smoke
Inhale me and I'll heighten your senses and take your mind to
new dimensions because as I mentioned

I'm dope!

*In life, people will try to marginalize you and place you into a neat
little box that makes them comfortable. Always remember who you
are and never compromise that for any person, job, or opportunity.
Your uniqueness is what will make you shine and set you apart
from others. Your gifts will make room for you.*

VOICE OF THE PEOPLE

I am the voice of the people
Getting to the point like the church's steeple
My thoughts are lethal
Giving birth to creativity
Hoping to spark minds with ingenuity
I speak the truth and I walk firm like I have something to prove
Can't give up on my people
That's why I preach and teach hoping that it may reach one of
you

SOUTHERN GIRL

I am a Southern girl.
I'm from the boot state.

You can taste the salt of the Gulf on my bootstraps.

I'm from where moss hugs the trees and hot summers tan your skin a sweet shade of molasses.

I'm a Southern girl who passes a slave plantation daily just to get home.

The irony of that dichotomy makes me stare at it every time I pass.

Envisioning times of the past.

Thinking of when, as a young child, I asked my grandmother what happened to her elbows.

She told me "They got this way picking cotton."

The thought of her doing any sort of slave labor always left a bad taste like something went rotten.

She explained how she would place that elbow on her knee as she stooped down to pick cotton from the bolls.

Then she showed me pictures of her mother with hair down to her waist and pictures of her grandfather with Indian feathers and paint on his face.

A Southern girl must know her past to understand what she can handle.

Do you see the army flag on the mantle? It was for my grandfather.
When he went to war, my grandmother bought this home.
A sweet little Southern estate that's all her own.

Pictures of all her babies on the wall with just enough room for a small garden out back and two fridges to store all of her Louisiana cuisines. A home with empty rooms ready to provide refuge to any of her children. This home is now our oasis; the one consistent thing in our family for generations.

My grandfather was a pastor who spoke the Gospel and tried to save souls. I still have a few of his sermons tucked away for when Southern days get too hot and take a toll. Days like when your temper flares as hot as the steam that comes from the ground after a Southern humid-filled rain. Leaving the concrete looking like someone placed dry ice on the pavement.

My mother is a calm spirit. She doesn't do much ranting and raving. Her patience with life drove her to be an educator who molds young minds.

My aunt is spicy like red cayenne and her strength is in her testimony.

I have an uncle, a military man, who has more books than a library. He reads law and history like the answers to the world's problems lie hidden in the text.

My oldest uncle was an electrician by trade but he broke a few barriers when he opened his store. He was an entrepreneur back when they weren't holding open the door.

My father was something like a brainiac. So smart he was often misunderstood. He moved away from Louisiana because the money was good. Went to fight in Vietnam and came home with a temper that stayed in a hurricane zone. A man with good intentions but in today's world, the good is hardly mentioned.

And me, I'm molded by people who don't run from storms. We take refuge until morning comes. I have a few family members who don't speak anymore because of past tensions.

See where I'm from, everyone likes to talk but no one likes to listen. I guess that's why I find solace in my paper and pen.

I am a Southern girl who knows where her ancestors have been.

I can be a little spicy at times but my aim isn't to fight. I get that flavor from knowing my elders' plight. If I hold on too tightly, just know that I'm doing this for my family. Who told me "It's ok to fall down but when you get up remember you are a winner and winners take all."

CHOSEN ONE

Don't be afraid to look me in my eyes
But borrow my ideas and forget you owe me
Discredit my thoughts but later you quote me
When you have no idea my potency

The ruthlessness of my mind has made some shiver
Some make idle promises but I deliver

My potency has been known to make some O.D.
The world will overdose on the real and swallow the fake
Lose sight of who you are and your purpose is at stake

Stay humble
Never fumble
And a world filled with trouble will never make you stumble

DEGREES

I'm deeper than a puddle so don't struggle trying to feel me
Often misunderstood so I guess it's in my pedigree

Some have more degrees than a thermostat
Recite facts from a book but lack continuity

Going to school and capitalizing on opportunity is nothing
new to me

Can't build only off of that so where is your ingenuity
I only deal with those who speak the real almost fluently

If you're not one of those you won't get close enough to
ruin me
My foundation wasn't built from accolades and graduations
but more from obstacles and situations

Remember that when you get to comparing degrees; you
can't measure me

I do not hang up every certificate nor do I highlight every
trial
Just feel my presence and know that I'm going to be here
for a while

Through
Christ...

EVERY DAY I'M SEARCHING

Every day and every day

I'm searching and I'm searching

For this bigger purpose, for this bigger picture

In this land where fairy tales don't exist and happy endings come seldom

Broken hearts and dead dreams are in abundance in the land that I live

Can't bask in happiness too long because around the corner lurks a problem and something seems to always be wrong

Through it all, I remain strong

Who knew finding my purpose would take so long

So every day and every day, I'm searching and searching

For this bigger purpose
For this bigger picture

Only to find out the key to my existence

Lives through Bible scriptures

I PRAY

Every day I pray......
I pray and pray......
Sometimes I pray when I don't know what to do

That's when I stop praying for myself and I start praying for you

BEAUTY
A Trip to the Beach

I saw the beauty in the land today

I saw the beauty in man today

I saw the beauty in my hands today

So I know that there must be beauty in me

HEY, LORD

Hey, Lord, I'm ready for my mission

I know that I was lost in the shuffle of life but now I am
ready to listen

Whatever the Lord sees fit for me that's what I will pursue

Let me know my path and purpose and that's what I will do

I will be committed to that and only that

No more obstacles slowing me down making me slow to
react
I am back and my talents I lay at your feet

Now tell me where I am needed and where to go

Because a man without a purpose is truly a lost soul

Without a mission rooted in spirituality and not just religion

One day your dreams may outweigh ambition

Therefore, you need the Lord beside you to give the
negativity some competition

That's why I am ready for my mission

I am ready to listen and give my purpose my attention

THIS TOO SHALL PASS

With God on your side, whom shall you fear?
When people use words as weapons shooting them like
arrows and carelessly slinging them like swords
The Lord is your shield
Slaying evildoers with their weapons at His will
The Lord is powerful and your wounds and insecurities He
shall heal
Just stay true to him during your trials and tribulations and
remain patient
Because this, too, shall pass.

Psalm 30:5 Weeping may endure for a night but joy
cometh in the morning

ANGEL

If everyone was created in your likeness, there would be
no wars and people's hearts would be absent of scars

If everyone was created in your likeness

You would be known as Your Highness to all and not just
to me
Because I worship the kindness of your heart and hope to
emulate thee

If the world was created in your likeness
The world would be absent of wickedness and everyone
would become righteous and stand for something even if it
meant standing alone
And everyone would have a home filled with love

If the world was created in your likeness, it might just be
heaven because you are above all
an angel here to give hope to those faced with turmoil and
danger
Don't ever change because a heart like yours is here to
give us a sample of what heaven is like

If it is in your likeness

POETIC
SOUL...

MY PEN IS NEVER RESTING

My pen writes the things that can only be composed in deep thought sessions

The things learned after life-altering lessons

The sins told to your priest yesterday in confession

My pen is never resting

My pen writes things that are on your mind resting but you fear releasing them because to some they may come across as vexing

My pen is never resting

The words of my pen get into your cerebellum like venom killing all preconceptions and releasing new conceptions

My pen's words make you break down your essence and figure out why you've been stressing

My pen is never resting

The words of pens are lethal like the weapon

Plotting potent booby traps throughout my poetry so watch where you are stepping

Embedding your footprints upon thoughts that crossed my mind once upon a time

As you read my poems line by line

I want you to feel enlightened and awakened

I'm not writing fiction but about modern-day tensions

Through my pen, I want to help cleanse the world of sin

I want the heavens and earth to sing the harmony sparked by my pen

My pen is never resting

POETIC SOUL

I need poetry to feed my soul
Without it, I just don't feel whole
Without poetry I'm incomplete
Therefore, I need poetry like a rapper needs a beat or like
humans need feet to generate mobility
Poems are my feet in the sense that they mobilize my
creativity
When I combine my words with my experiences, they take
flight
Taking a simple statement to new heights
I have a poetic soul
It's like words take hold of my mind and those words and
ideas combine to make a masterpiece that's all mine
I guess it's safe to say that I have the soul of a poet and I
know it and like a true poet I keep on flowing

MY SONG

You can't stop my music because with or without you, it
goes on
You can take my radio but you can't take away "my song
that I will hum in my head"

From the minute my feet hit the floor to the second my
head hits the bed

I move to the beat of life

I orchestrate my own anthem

You can move to my beat if you wish but I suggest you
make your own noise and dance to your own music

You may try to take me off my rhythm

Making me lose count but I will not forget how to follow my
notes because at the end of the day I know what kind of
song I want

I want a song of victory

One of inspiration

A song that motivates others through desperation

A song that tells of a testimony that started with harsh
pitches but ends with sweet melodic harmonies

That's my song

PROLIFIC ORATOR EVOKING THOUGHT – P.O.E.T.

I am a prolific orator evoking thought

Convincing your mind to think about things it ought

Emancipating your intellect

For years you've slept

Now your mind is awakened

Shaken from the slumber you fell under

You wonder how your mind stayed shackled so long

Like slaves with freedom papers

You somehow forgot that you were free

Using material things to define you made your existence in vain

So, the gifts inside of you were slain for pieces of fortune and fame

WHAT IS
LOVE...

WHAT HAPPENS TO A LOVE?

What happens to a love that couldn't be or shouldn't be?
The more you reach for it, the farther away it gets

Does it cease to exist or fall into a black abyss?
Or does it make your heart hard as a clenched fist?

What happens to a love that couldn't be or shouldn't be?
But you still want it like the air you breathe
The more you inhale the more it flees
Does it ever leave or does it take shelter in all its old memories?

What happens to a love that couldn't be or shouldn't be?
The more you think you've got it in your grasp
The faster it runs and the harder it laughs

What happens to a love that couldn't be or shouldn't be, when you realize its inability?

Does it laugh at your humility, making you lower your standards and increase your vulnerability?

What happens to a love that can't be?
Does it ever capsize or sink?

Or does it forever live on between your thoughts, between your blinks
Between your heartbeats

What happens when the love that couldn't meet the love that can? Will it all make sense then? What happens?

LOVING YOU

In my life, I've seen many things fall apart

I've seen smiles turn into frowns and people wounded by broken hearts

I've been hurt
I've been confused
I've been lost

I've been alone but when I look into your eyes I feel like I've found my home

My soul has found its mate and all the tears were worth the wait

THE GOD IN YOU

I love the God in you

How when the chips are down I can always find the Lord in you I love that when I'm in my darkest hours you greet me with scriptures

Turning my negative outlook into a positive picture

With you, I know that someone is always praying for me

I love your silence when you pause from the world to talk to God
Your constant dialogue with Him allows me to trust our trials and embrace the journey

Because I know now that worrying isn't for me if I trust in Him In a world filled with confusion, I am glad the Lord sent me you and blessed our union

Hey, mama, why don't you smile anymore

Do you remember those loud shoulder-shaking laughs, those giggles that lit the entire room, or that smirk that stole hearts before words were even exchanged

Can you tell me when it all changed?

The day your smile was washed away with the rain of tears of pain

Placing a cloud over your sunny days

Now all that remains is the imprint of what could have been

What can I do to restore your smile?

I know that I'm just your child but I think it is vile for you to deprive us of the warmth of your heart

Because it is you who lifts me when I am down but who's going to wipe away your frown

I want you to laugh until your belly aches and you begin to cry

Cry those tears of joy

I want you to smile like a child who just got a new toy on Christmas day

I wonder who stole my mother's smile away

I crave for your heart to fill back up with love so I can see you smile again

Then I can know the true meaning of happiness and believe that
life can be good for good people

I just want your heart to sing of bliss because I have almost
forgotten how delightful your smile is

I look at old pictures to reminisce because I need your smile like
the Egyptians need the Nile to replenish their crops. So, I pray
for your smile before my smile stops

I need you to smile soon so I can see that happiness and your
smile prevailed and the harshness of the world failed

So I can believe that happy endings do exist and that life isn't as
hard as a clenched fist
and after the storm, there is bliss

At the beginning and end of each day, it is your smile that I miss

I close this poem with a kiss longing for your laugh to live on and
manifest through this period of darkness

Which is only a test that upon completing God will bless you with
a permanent radiant smile that is so bright it competes with the
rays of the sunlight

Mama, Just Smile

*This poem is about kids raised in a single-parent household who saw
their mother/father do everything in their power to give them a good life.
In some cases, parents sacrifice their happiness for their children. In
this poem, I reflected on a time in my childhood when my mother
worked miles away from our city to provide for her family but she never
complained. However, I knew she wasn't happy. She put our happiness
above her own.*

FATHER'S STATE OF MIND (A CONVERSATION)

Sometimes I feel like I have my Father's state of mind:
"Ain't got time to talk so you better fall in line
May not like me but you will respect my grind"

The world owes me nothing but I'm still going for what is mine
Searching for the truth in people but it's hard to find

A young person with an old soul
If you're looking for me to lose, remember I may bend but I never fold

I can hear my Father say to me
"Don't take any wooden nickels, baby girl

Stay focused and do not be conformed to this world.
Remember it's mind over matter

Put your faith and family first and let the rest come after
And I know sometimes the road gets tough

Just remember you are built for this so never give up
Know that you have me upstairs rooting for you every time you look up at the sky
Since I left you
I never left your side

I know some may not have the best things to say about me
when they hear my name

Just know that I made mistakes but most people don't
leave the earth the way they came
I gave to my kids all that I had and although my life on
earth was not long

I know that through me my kids were made strong"

Dad, what is understood doesn't need to be explained
I learned a long time ago that you can never please man
I never thought you went away because I feel your
presence every day
I get the signs you send to me when I am alone
I just hope you are proud of me when you look down

YOU ARE

You are the beat behind a beautiful song

Even when the vocalist stops you are still there making your presence known

The beauty of your heart is like the Egyptian pyramids and the cathedrals of Rome

I'm happy to call your heart my home

RELEASE ME

Release me from this love that I feel
This love that I know can't be and never will
Release me so I can have a breath of freedom and
understand why
this love should have never come
You love from a heart that is filled with pain and the love I
give in return is not the same
I feel our love is imprisonment of which I will never be set
free
Trapped is what I feel when I think of me and you

So, I'll let you go now

And you release me

I DO

I Love you; I swear I Do
But how can I love when I don't have a clue
Those who loved me truly were only a few
Most of my life has been filled with replacing people who
were supposed to play a role
Now that you are here how do I relinquish control?

DNA: TOXICITY O F LOVE

Have you ever been around someone and you catch their
negativity like a cold or a bug?

Creeping into your bloodstream killing dreams

Altering your DNA

Now you doubt the honest and wonder if there are any genuine
people amongst us

As the negativity spreads through your body like a fungus

Clinging to you like a parasite

Sucking out love, peace, happiness, and drive

Secretly hoping you never regain your splendor

Leaving you confused, weak, and limber

Until you decide to fight back and deny the foreign substance in
your blood and surrender

Now your antibodies have developed a shield

You know now that you must remove the toxic parasite for you to
live

Angering the virus because it was content with the destructive relationship

It blames you for the transformed state of the habitat and complaints because it can no longer control you through your capillaries and veins

Then, you finally get your diagnosis and realize it was family that caused you all this pain

The fake hugs

 The disingenuous love

When you secretly pray for my downfall and hope that I don't win Calling yourself family and friends

The smiles you give to my face and the blank stares you give as I walk away

These are a few of the reasons why I consider you a snake

The way you hate to acknowledge my successes is the reason why I never tell you my blessings

Should you ever wonder why I can't pretend when it's convenient

Just remember all the venom and the artificial love that was given

AMERICA...

OBAMA - After the Election Results

Rosa Parks sat so Martin could walk
Martin walked so Obama could run
Obama ran so we can fly[2]
Fly beyond the past political disenfranchisement and
economic exploitation
To end the frustration of prolonged wars and restore peace
A peace that is now as much mine as it is theirs

I can vote and know that the outcome will be fair
See, Obama, you've awakened the soul
The soul of a country whose hope had lost its flair
A nation whose past turmoil soiled the hands and futures
of many Now this country can cleanse itself and dream
Can you send a message to Martin that we made it to the
Promised Land?

Tell him that we did it just as he planned Together with
Blacks and Whites hand-in-hand
Now color no longer defines me and I can truly be anything
I want to be
Mediocrity takes the backseat as I recognize the realness
of possibilities

Tell Malcolm that we did it with all religions aligned
To remove the negativity from the White House and the
pain-stained memories of struggle from our minds
No one died in vain, no slaves' labor was in vain

YES, WE CAN! And yes, we did Yes, I can, and yes, I will

---

[2] Jay-Z

STOP! DON'T SHOOT

We, too, sing America

We are just of a darker creation but we, too, bleed the
blood of this nation

Our blood runs deep
In the soil
In the crops
In the trees
In Billie Holiday's Strange Fruit dangling in the breeze
The reality is we are free but still afraid of the sirens and
blue suits
Black skin does not mean criminal nor crook

We are educated taxpayers, and law-abiding citizens.
However, all that is masked because we are preceded by
our skin

Stop don't shoot

We are Fathers, Mothers, Daughters, and Sons Not just
some prey you kill and hunt

It's no surprise that we have to keep reminding this country
that equality and equity are still factors and that do BLACK
LIVES MATTER

How many more splatters of blood-stained sidewalks have
to be made

Before America's hatred fades

WHAT IS LIBERTY?

Life, liberty, and the pursuit of happiness were the
foundation on which this country was made and the reason
why many people still come to America today

Truth be told those liberties seem to only exist on paper
and America treats most people of color as if they are
doing us some kind of favor

When the land they write rules to control was built from the
blood sweat and tears of their darker neighbors

Whose labor was in vain because what we built, we can't
stake a claim or seek to obtain

Now most of us live under a strain

Can't have the land we built because the rules were not
written for us or by us

Contrary to the belief of democracy

There is no equality in the land that I see

Now we sit back and watch others rise to fame when we
were robbed of our heritage and tamed like beasts

Taught that anything having to do with our African heritage was nothing to keep

However, when we walked on African soil, we had diamonds and gold underneath our feet

Kings and queens to meet, and moors that traveled the world to teach

America's Liberty needs glasses

She's been blind so long I wonder if she will ever get past it

BLACK PANTHER

I'm hungry like a black panther

Some say I'm militant but trying to label me is not the answer

Most people fear what they don't understand

So, in life, I'm not looking to have many fans

Screaming by any means necessary

I'm never casting down my bucket

Marching through the streets, fist-pumping, causing much ruckus

I would rather invest in another Talented Tenth

With hopes that they could help this generation get some sense

Because the crisis is we don't know what our vices are

And no, I don't have the antidote but I do recognize what the problem is

However, it takes more than one to solve it

Too many years of being miseducated caused it

Yes, I am hungry like a black panther

Starved by the hopes of an American Dream

Preceded by my color it seems which explains this
unquenchable thirst

Doomed from creation with this so-called Black Curse

Starving in a country that is supposed to provide equality
and liberty for all

Trying to get a piece of that American Pie

For the cause of righteousness how many people have to
die

Hoping that the American Dream isn't just another lie

POSITIVE

I just want to hear something positive
Some dry-your-eyes-it's-gonna-be-alright talk
With all the negative that happens every day

I just want to hear some 'God hears you when you pray

Lay your head down in comfort because God has you
covered in your weakest moments

These days, families don't get along and houses aren't
homes but I want to hear "Big Mama's cooking. Come
over"
You don't have to be alone

All the negativity is killing my creativity

I just want to hear something positive so I can sit and think
about how good God is and count my blessings

I just want to hear something positive
 Like "I got you this just because it's all love."

There's way too much hate in the world today and some
are succumbing to it but me

I just want to hear something positive

BLACK GIRL MAGIC

You move with a grace that is all your own

Throwing caution to the wind as you struggle to hold on to your crown
Skin shades black as coal and eyes that have seen stories untold
Ole Mother of Man
Sister of the Struggle

Civilizations and families have been built on your back They ostracize you to hide that you are a living artifact
A Goddess A Queen
An echo of ancient empires that reigned supreme

You are a rebirth of strength personified through your wit and the uncanny way manages to overcome
Isolating the pains caused by the iniquities of the world to fulfill your obligations and responsibilities for your families
Anyone else staring adversity in the eye daily would be a wreck but you hold it together with your black girl magic
A magic that makes tragic scars disappear and one that digests fears

It is through you that life manifested
You are something like the cure
Pure 100% Proof
The truth

Leaving your footprints on the world
A young Black girl rising from the ashes
Removing slave lashes
Kemet blood flowing through your veins
Your ancestry left stains so your brain is elevated
Looking towards the future but your thoughts are slightly
antiquated
Never forgetting from where you came
Not searching for fame but change or to spark the mind that
changes the land
That is your plan
You are MAGIC
From your curly hair to your full lips, and the curve of your hips
you have been uniquely created
Made to be unapologetically resilient
You are perfectly imperfect
Finally realizing you are worth it
Now you can take back your crown and have your seat on the
throne
With a feeling of familiarity that lets you know you were destined
for greatness all along and that your Black Girl Magic led you
home

AMERICA

I'm sick of the same old narrative
A new story is imperative
I'm sick of the same old characters
Good cop, bad cop - they're still killing us

America has never been feeling us
Always trying to put hate and fear in us
Watch the news constantly just smearing us
Always showing us in fisticuffs
Hardly ever show those uplifting us
Trayvon made it clear to us
But not guilty? That's mysterious
The red, white, and blue not hearing us
Downplaying slavery is ridiculous
Those 400 years made a difference

Some say that we have the curse of Ham
Accept that and you'll be damned

Join the war teamed up with Uncle Sam
Thinking that it will make you a part of the fam
Got home and found out it was all a sham

Because America has never been feeling us

Always trying to put hate and fear in us
Bend the rules and laws now they're killing us

Take our art and culture because it's priceless

Fight back and they will label you too righteous but I'll fight back until I'm lifeless

Got the world thinking it's all about Isis but America is in a black and white crisis
Undermine our people just to spite us
Still inflicted by our vices

HIP HOP...

DUMB

I'm dumb with it
Just having fun with it
Drop a bar with a pun it
Then I run with it
Lyrical like slum village
I'm Illmatic until the casket
Wearing my black girl magic like Baduizm
Wrapping your head with euphemisms
Positive affirmations give me the patience to pimp a
butterfly while I'm waiting
Waiting on better days but my name isn't Pac
Still cutting corners on my childhood block
Investing in myself like a stock
My word is bond
If I say it you better set your alarm

HIP HOP

I want to become one with Hip-Hop so it can live in my soul

So, the ruthless rhythm of the rhyme can live at my
fingertips and the boldly beautiful beats can live at my toes

As the volume grows, my body loses control, and in
seconds the music wraps, taps, taps, and snaps my mind,
and my thoughts are left inclined and through the dark
haze of the musical maze

I find myself enlightened and amazed by the lyricist's ways
of verbal expression

Each bar is a new lesson

THE STORY OF A SELL-OUT - (WHEN HIP HOP GOES MAINSTREAM)

WAR
WAR

We go to war for reasons that are unknown
America fights for other countries when our country is a
complete war zone
Blacks vs Whites
Whites vs Blacks

The truth of the matter is it's not only about color anymore
It's about who can get the riches the fastest

How you do this does not matter
Just as long as you change your economic status

As a result, we have so many rappers
Who just want a piece of the American Pie
So, is it really their fault
To single out one would be opening a vault

When who am I to judge and point fingers when I too am a
slave to the cash collection cult

I not going to sprinkle salt on the game
Let them have their fame

I'd rather have them on video sets than on the block selling
cocaine or from the impoverished streets of the ghetto from
which so many of them came

Why hate the brother he ain't to blame

He only saw a gate open and snuck in
Not thinking of the long-term effects of selling your soul
and compromising your integrity for fifteen minutes in the
spotlight and a life of temptation and sin

Now he's a statistic
They got him believing the hype
He got the big head, never saw him as the selling-out type
I guess everyone has a price

Couldn't stay Hood Chic forever
Got tired of keeping his ghetto ties to the poor
Peeking into the back door of the wealthy
Commercialized himself and his lyrics now his bank
account is healthy

This is the story of a sellout
Who couldn't see because he was blinded by the clout

Had he stayed true to himself instead of the dollar he
wouldn't have lost his route
No doubt he is being pimped by his record label who is a
slave to the media

And the media are mere puppets as they dance to get
ratings from their demographics

Got him fiending for sales like an addict
Soon, his album sold out everywhere and so did his soul
He found out that he was the toll to be paid for fortune and
fame

Couldn't have it all
Got the money but lost the sincerity of his name

THE STORM…

THE BATTLE

I am a soldier
No, I didn't enlist in any army but I drag myself from the
depths of despair
To face the cruel and mean world every morning
No, I'm not ducking bullets or dodging bombs

I'm just hiding in the trenches of life waiting for a better day
to come

I am a soldier and every day I get suited up with all the
weapons I need for successful combat because life takes a
lot of prisoners and some of them don't come back
So, I refuse to be another casualty of war
I have won too many battles and came too far

Yes, I am a soldier
No army fatigue or medals needed

Anything worth having is worth fighting for
You must take heed
Life requires blood sweat and tears to succeed

LIFE

Nobody cares, little girl
Didn't you learn that when you were younger
Life takes good people and turns them into monsters

Nobody cares, little girl

So, dry your eyes and put on your armor because today's
struggle has nothing on what I have planned for tomorrow

Nobody cares, little girl

Life will eat your dreams for breakfast
Devour your passions by lunch
And consume you by dinner

See life can be crazy and it will do anything so that you
won't be a winner

Have you worried, stressing, and getting thinner

Nobody cares, little girl

I think you get it now, little sister
Life will turn your positive perspective into a negative
picture

BEAUTY FOR YOUR ASHES

I am stronger now that I've made it through the storm
I can finally sit back and watch my dreams take full form
My enemies did not want to see me stand tall
So, I got down on my knees and prayed
Now the holes they dug for me
in them
they will fall

Walking in the divinity of His grace makes any obstacle
easier to face
That is why I stand strong in my faith because if it were not
for the Lord I would've lost this race

"I can do all things through Christ who strengthens me"

Philippians 4:13

MY SOUL

I have a soul that never dies

Even in the mists of a storm my soul never subsides
Adversity only summons the fighter in me to rise

Never knew I embodied so much strength until the valleys
came So, I laced up my boots and endured rain but I came
to the top of the mountain with newfound courage which
awakened a wisdom that shakes walls and courage that
makes evildoers fall

Like Daniel in the lion's den

My soul makes me like an alien among most men
With a dream in my head and God in my heart
I am ready for life's most ruthless wars

With a soul and spirit that never shakes nor falters, I
consider myself one of life's truest martyrs

HUNGRY

I'm hungry but not for food but for what most minds elude

I'm hungry for a renewed mood and a rebirth of a vibe

Like why am I live

What purpose did He place inside of me before I occupied
my mother's womb

For what did the Lord see when He made me and gave me
these brown eyes

Did He carefully devise my fires knowing that I would
always come out alive

Did He strategically place my obstacles so that I may gain
strength by moving the boulders

Did He carefully orchestrate the placement of my
distractions to watch my reaction

Waiting to know when I was ready to unlock my purpose
that lay dormant because I did not know how to feed this
hunger

TIRED

Sometimes I get tired of being me
Maybe if I wasn't me, I could be all that I can be
My pain coupled with my insecurities paralyze my every
thought of greatness
As my purpose dies a million deaths in the depths of my
solitude
Life is crude
People are crass
As I struggle to live fighting for every gasp
Living a life where your face laughs but your heart cries
This is the mask I wear because it seems most people are
too busy to care

SICK

I'm so sick of everything associated with life
From waking up in the mornings to going to bed at night
To the trivial conversations, you have with people just to be polite
I'm so tired of people feasting on everything I embody until all that remains of me is a body
I'm tired of playing the hand I've been dealt so most of the time I'm crying out for help
Then I remember that even Jesus wept
I'm sick of love that is as fragile as two tiny hands binding together to sing and make the London Bridge that seems to always fall down
I'm tired of wearing a crown but never finding my throne

AN ODE TO TROUBLED SOULS

This is an ode to troubled souls

Who on the outside look young but on the inside they're old
Because their pain has festered so long that it has made calluses from the many times the bad memories rub against their hearts and reopen the wounds in their brains

This is an ode to troubled souls who may sleep but who never really rest because when they close their eyes the weight of their journey lies heavily on their chests

With a mind that is strong enough to make it through the day but at night the pain stalks them like shadows on the walls

This is an ode to troubled souls who were once filled with so much joy and optimism but now feel cold

No one ever has the answers when the problems are astronomical

No one ever has the answers when the pain is insurmountable

WONDER

Sometimes I wonder if I will ever be truly happy again on earth

It's like I'm here and I feel so alone and so out of place
To be in contact with people who I feel no likeness makes life hard

It makes having a conversation hard
Being open hard
It makes trusting hard

I'm constantly learning to be an outsider inside myself
I feel incomplete most of the time
Like a shell of something that once was

Because you're gone

GET UP! – I WON'T BE DEFEATED (A MOMENT IN TIME)

The day I died I thought everything I was taught as a child was a lie.

I was taught to pray, walk a righteous path, give to those who are less fortunate, and respect my marriage vows.

My mother said to treat others the way you want to be treated but somehow on that day I still got cheated.

The day I died I somehow found myself lying lifeless on a hospital bed ready to surrender.

I was strapped to an EKG machine to monitor my heart that I knew would never beat the same again.

Suddenly I heard Bang, Bang, and Clang. The sounds of a walking cane hitting the cold pale hospital floors.

Then I heard "Where is she?" "Take me to her room" the voice echoed through the hall.

When I opened my swollen tear-filled eyes the shadow of my grandmother appeared on the wall.

She sat in the chair closest to my bed and waited patiently until every doctor and relative left the room. Then she bent over my hospital bed and said "Get Up! You get up right now! You still got work to do."

It was at that moment I felt myself take that one breath to fight. It was like she was speaking to my spirit. At that moment she gave me a piece of her strength.

I knew then I couldn't quit.

Looking at her strength as a child had given me the blueprint I needed on my path to resiliency.

God gave her to me for such a time as this.

I set up, clenched my fist, and prepared to fight.

LISTEN...

KEEPING IT REAL

Big chains and diamond rings
Flashy cars and shiny things
Gives us the impression of being kings

We make a hobby out of buying things we can't afford
While others save up and buy the house on the hill with the
multiple floors

We blow all our cash on outrageous fads seen on rap
stars' videos and blow the other half on equipment for car
stereos

No college funds for us because we live in the present
Forget stocks and bonds or any other forms of investments
because I have to buy a new truck "limited edition"

Priorities wrong, money gone

Left all alone with material things that are priceless once
you open them up or put them on

That's as far as our money goes but nothing beats that
feeling
Fresh new suit, shiny shoes, hopping out of a car that
makes everyone stop and look

These are the things Blacks took instead of bettering
ourselves from the inside out

We continue wearing our opinion of ourselves on our overpriced sleeves

Once we take off our expensive clothes our high self-esteem leaves

Can you believe this is the price we pay from being enslaved physically one day

To being enslaved mentally the next

This has got to be a hex because little do you know, you just paid for another man to send his daughter to college or invest in his community

When all you got out of the deal was some new kicks, he stretched his money far enough to feed a family of six

What can we do to fix the fact that we as a people do not know how to save money and invest in our potential Thereby never creating a new tomorrow

One where clothes and other material things aren't the only ways to indicate power

True power lies underneath your new Jordan's, Fendi, Gucci, and fresh Tim's

Stop letting your clothes make you and let you make them
because underneath your clothes you must have a
personality, an identity, and a skill

Yeah, girl, you look good but is that all you have to offer to
the world? I hope not

But if so, you have a lot to learn because you just spent
your last dime on a designer purse and now you don't have
any money to put into it

So, watch where your money goes or make sure it doesn't
benefit someone or something you want to oppose

Matter of fact just keep your wallet closed

Feed your mind and one day you will know what's worth
your last dime

TIME KEEPS MOVING

Time keeps moving and to keep from losing you've got to keep moving, too

Choosing your next position with precision
Hoping you've made the right decision
Keeps you on your toes

So, your mind is never fully rested but that's the way life goes I'm just getting started and the things on my mind have already harvested into full-grown problems & obsessions

From my future goals and profession to the need to have material possessions

So, when you are resting
I'm plotting my next move
Just getting started so I'm finding my groove
Finding out how to take ideas from the atmosphere to the earth
For all to feel

Life is real
It's not a game like Monopoly or Charades
In life, you have to play to keep from getting played

LOYALTY

My loyalty to some has come and gone but for those, I still cling to
There isn't anything I wouldn't do

Finding someone real in a world filled with fakes is like finding a diamond in the rubble of an earthquake
Something valuable should be treasured
To lose it goes beyond measure

MY CITY
Baton Rouge- An Ode to the Summer of 2016- The Red Summer

Too much pain in my city
Murder rate going up
Now it seems to always rain in my city 2016 will always be
ingrained in my city

That year Red Stick took on a new meaning in my city
The blood and flood of that summer will forever stay in the
veins of my city

Homes being remodeled and no police convictions echo
through the plains of my city
You have to stay focused because you can lose your
brains in my city
Too many people manipulating and playing games in my
city
That's why it's hard to stay sane in my city
Police harass you for nothing in my city
One false move and you are just another name in my city
Sometimes you have to isolate yourself from the masses to
maintain in my city
Not acting differently just trying to stay alive and remain on
the streets of my city
If you have a family to feed don't look for pity in my city

Taking a loss and being able to bounce back is how you
make it in my city

Stay down too long don't expect somebody to help you up
in my city

It takes a combination of book smarts and being gritty to
survive my city

Many move away because it's hard to win in my city
If you are not built for this, forget you ever came to my city

BLACK SOULS

Tic-toc do you hear the clock
Time waits for no man
It seems that you need a plan

Too many times before, people have lied and tried to lead
you astray

That's why you pray to keep those with black souls away
Those who can drown light or dreams like black holes or
like a match swallowed by an abyss

Those who are as empty on the inside as the liquor bottle
they clench

They seek to step on every inch of hope you seem to
muster up because years ago, they couldn't hack it so they
gave up

You pray to keep those with black souls away

Those who seek to lynch your dreams because theirs
didn't survive

Now they try to place limits on how you rise because they
fear your potential and envy your drive

WAKE UP!

Constitution, constitution, where is our retribution

Will we as people ever win or are we forever destined to keep losing

Choosing mediocrity because the American Dream is a lot harder for us it seems

Because we have to be better than the best
Rise to every occasion
Pass every test

Anything less will ultimately put us in a category with those who can care less

Those who are more obsessed with outer appearances than with mental advances

Every day they are missing out on chances
And most of the time opportunity knocks only once

While you're out having fun someone has already taken your chance, your spot, and your position

So, it's time to wake up and listen

Being young is not an excuse to keep missing THE POINT!

Quotes and Word Play

Perspective
From my perspective things are hectic but you have been spoon-fed so you have become blinded by your blessings

Overcomer
You ever have days when you are just tired but you don't know what you are tired from
Then you remember all the things you've overcome

Defeat
Have you ever looked defeat in the eyes and said you refuse to die because "the devil is a lie"

Word walls
I've always been told if you don't have anything good to say then you should say nothing at all.
That's why I'm trapped in my word walls that were built from all the things left unsaid

P.T.S.D. (Post-Traumatic Stress Disorder)
Everybody wants me to win but deep in my heart   I feel it's over
Every time I get close to happiness
I look over my shoulder

Chosen

Lord have mercy on my soul
Sometimes I feel like my heart has turned cold
And my soul has vacated my body and I was never told
What role am I supposed to play in a world that denounces
me because the Lord isn't ready to announce the anointing
he bestowed upon me
I'm made to walk with men who don't recognize who sent
me